Amazing Animal Hunters

TIGERS

Sally Morgan

amicus

Published by Amicus
P.O. Box 1329, Mankato, Minnesota 56002

Printed in the United States of America at Corporate Graphics, in North Mankato, Minnesota.

Library of Congress Cataloging-in-Publication Data
Morgan, Sally.
 Tigers / by Sally Morgan.
    p. cm. -- (Amazing animal hunters)
 Includes index.
 Summary: "Discusses the life of tigers and profiles different types of tigers, along with providing facts
about habitat, hunting practices, diet, and more. Also includes records on tigers"--Provided by publisher.
 ISBN 978-1-60753-049-7 (library binding)
 1. Tigers--Juvenile literature. I. Title.
 QL737.C23M6696 2011
 599.756--dc22

                                                                                    2009048515

Created by Q2AMedia
Editor: Katie Dicker
Art Director: Harleen Mehta
Designers: Shruti Aggarwal, Tarang Saggar
Picture Researcher: Sujatha Menon

All words in **bold** can be found in the Glossary on pages 30–31.

Picture credits
t=top b=bottom c=center l=left r=right
Cover images: Ludmila Yilmaz/Shutterstock,Roman Kobzarev/Istockphoto

Andrea Poole/Istockphoto: Title page, Artur Tiutenko/Shutterstock: Contents page, John Hyde/Photolibrary: 4, Estima/Fotolia: 5t,
Shutterstock: 5b, Andy Rouse/NHPA: 6, Pillai Balan/Istockphoto: 7t, Photolibrary: 7b, Satyendra Tiwari/Ecoscene: 8,
Andrea Poole/Istockphoto: 9, Pradeep Kumar Saxena/Istockphoto: 10, Max Earey/Shutterstock: 11t, Ken Brown/Istockphoto: 11b,
Stefan Ekernas/Istockphoto: 12, Mike Dabell/Istockphoto: 13t, Brian Opyd/Istockphoto: 13b, Andy Rouse/NHPA: 14,
Mahipal Singh/Photolibrary: 15, Sigge/Dreamstime: 16, Megan Lorenz/Istockphoto: 17, Steve Geer/Istockphoto: 18,
Chris Sargent/Shutterstock: 19t, Phillip Cola/Ecoscene: 19b, Ludmia Yimaz/Shutterstock: 20, Kane/Shutterstock: 21t,
Ludmila Yilmaz/Shutterstock: 21b, Photolibrary: 22, Dale Robert Franz/Photolibrary: 23, John Moore/AP Photos: 24,
Parth Sanyal/Reuters: 25t, Jayanta Shaw/Reuters: 25b, Satyendra Tiwari/Ecoscene: 26, Karl Ammann/Ecoscene: 27,
Michael Steden/Istockphoto: 28, Nick Biemans/Istockphoto: 29, Steve Geer/Istockphoto: 31.

DAD0043
42010

9 8 7 6 5 4 3 2 1

Contents

King of the Cats

Tigers are the largest cats on Earth. Their orange fur and dark stripes make them easy to recognize. These powerful hunters have large, sharp teeth and claws. It is no surprise that they are called the king of the cats.

Types of Tigers

Tigers are **mammals**, a type of animal that is covered in hair. The females feed their young with milk. Their closest relatives are the lion, leopard, and cheetah. There is only one kind, or **species**, of tiger. But tigers that live in different parts of the world look different. Scientists divide them into types according to where they are found. There is the Bengal or Indian, Siberian, Indo-Chinese, Malay, Sumatran, and South China tiger. Three other types—the Balinese, Caspian, and Javan—are sadly now **extinct**.

The Siberian tiger is the largest tiger of all. It runs through the snow on its big, padded paws.

Tiger Culture

Tigers are important characters in some cultures. In China, the tiger represents strength and power. It is one of the 12 animals of the Chinese **zodiac**. The tiger is the national animal of India and Bangladesh. There are many statues and paintings of tigers around the world, and in some places there are tiger festivals.

Large eyes to see prey

Rounded head supports tiger's strong jaws

Tigers are well known for their stripes, which can be brown, dark gray, or black.

SIGN OF THE KING

The pattern of stripes on the forehead of a tiger can look like the Chinese character that means "king." 王

In China, the tiger is also thought to be lucky. These tigers decorate the wall of a Chinese temple.

Powerful Hunters

A tiger is built for hunting. Its muscular body can run, leap, and jump, while its teeth and claws grip and rip flesh apart. The stripes are important too, providing perfect **camouflage**.

Rippling Muscles

Tigers are large—the largest weighs more than 772 pounds (350 kg)—but they can move quickly over short distances, powered by their strong muscles. A fully-grown tiger can leap more than 9 yards (8 m) or scale a 6.5 foot (2 m) high tree. Their shoulders and front legs are heavily muscled and are used to knock a **prey** animal to the ground, then carry it away. The hook-shaped claws grip onto the prey to stop it from escaping.

 A tiger's back legs are longer than the front legs, which is ideal for running, jumping, and pouncing.

Powerful shoulder muscles

A tiger's orange fur with black stripes blends well with long grass.

Perfect Camouflage

Tigers have more than 100 stripes, which are useful for camouflage. The stripes break up the shape of the tiger's body, making it difficult for prey animals to spot them. When a tiger stands in the forest or lies down in long grass, it virtually disappears. This allows a tiger to creep up on its prey.

The longest claw is about 4.7 inches (12 cm) long

Curved claws for gripping

UNIQUE MARKINGS

Tiger stripes vary in length, width, and number and are like fingerprints—no two tigers have the same pattern. This helps scientists to identify individual animals.

Tigers pull their claws back into a protective sheath when not in use so they stay sharp.

Tiger Territory

Less than 100 years ago, tigers roamed across much of Central, South, and Southeast Asia as far west as Turkey. Now they are only found in parts of South and Southeast Asia, and in a few forested areas of Eastern Russia and China.

Jungle Homes

Each of the different types of tiger lives in a particular **habitat**. The Bengal, Indo-Chinese, Malay, and Sumatran tigers are found in **jungles**. A jungle, or rain forest, is a dense forest found in areas with a **tropical** climate. The temperatures are high all year round, and there is a lot of rain. Tigers spend much of the day resting beside pools and streams. Sometimes they stand in the water to keep cool. Not surprisingly, they are strong swimmers.

 Unlike other cats, tigers like to be near water.

Chilly Forests

The Siberian tiger lives to the north, in the mountainous regions of Northern China and Eastern Russia, where there are huge pine forests. This tiger has to cope with the extreme winter weather when temperatures fall way below freezing, the ground is covered in deep snow, and the rivers are frozen.

CASPIAN TIGER

The Caspian tiger, which is now extinct, was found in Central Asia and as far west as Turkey. In the twentieth century, the tiger was hunted, and its forest home was cleared to grow cotton and rice.

The Siberian tiger has to survive the extreme cold of the Siberian winter.

9

The Bengal Tiger

The Bengal, or Indian, tiger is probably the best known of all tigers. It is the evil tiger, Shere Khan, featured in the movie *The Jungle Book*.

Powerful Hunter

The Bengal tiger is found in tropical jungle, in open forest, and even in mangrove swamps along the coast. Small numbers are found in Nepal, Bhutan, and Myanmar. As top **predator** of the forest, it is not hunted by other animals. A powerful animal of about 10 feet (3 m) in length from nose to tail and weighing up to 440 pounds (200 kg), it can kill large animals. It eats mostly wild deer, but will also take wild pigs, birds, and even the gaur, a type of buffalo.

The Bengal tiger is often found near rivers or shady pools.

White Tigers

Rare white Bengal tigers have a white fur with pale stripes. There are several hundred white tigers living in zoos. They are mostly descendents of a white tiger called Mohan caught in India in 1951. White tigers tend to grow faster and become heavier than the normal orange Bengal tiger.

 White Bengal tigers have pale stripes on white fur and bright blue eyes.

Save the Tigers

The Bengal tiger is under threat. Huge areas of its forest home have been cleared, and tigers have been killed by **poachers**. A century ago there were 40,000 Bengal tigers roaming the Indian forests, but now there are thought to be fewer than 1,400.

During the 1970s, the Indian government set up Project Tiger and created new tiger **reserves** across the country. **Conservation** organizations such as the WWF (World Wildlife Fund) worked to save the tiger, too. During the 1990s, numbers rose to more than 3,000, but, unfortunately, things started to go wrong. As poaching increased, tigers disappeared from some reserves. Poaching is difficult to control and is still a major threat to the Bengal tiger.

भारत
INDIA

25
1975

जिम कार्बेट शताब्दी
1875-1955
JIM CORBETT CENTENARY

 The Bengal tiger is the national symbol of India and Bangladesh.

Tiger Food

Tigers are **carnivores**, which means they have a meat diet. They hunt and eat other animals. Their sharp teeth and claws are shaped to slice through flesh, and they use their powerful limbs to chase and trap prey.

Time for a Feast

One of the favorite prey animals of the Bengal tiger is the chital deer, which weighs about 154 pounds (70 kg). Each year, a tiger needs to eat about 70 chital deer (or the equivalent weight in other animals). The tiger's habitat must have plenty of food to support it. If the tiger kills too many deer and they die out, it will lose an important source of food. Tigers prey on other creatures, too, such as monkeys, birds, badgers, bears, frogs, and even insects. The tiger kills and eats almost any animal it can get its paws on. It also eats rotting meat and fruit.

The chital deer is also called the spotted deer because of its white spots.

A Powerful Bite

There are 30 teeth in a tiger's mouth. The small incisors at the front are used for gripping and nibbling meat off bones. The four dagger-like **canines** (two at the top and two at the bottom) are used to grip and kill prey. The premolars and molars that lie behind the canines are large teeth that slice meat into chunks the tiger can swallow.

The upper canine is about 4 inches (10 cm) long, the size of a man's finger.

GIANT MEALS

A tiger may go for days without eating, so it gorges itself when it kills. A hungry tiger can eat almost one-fifth of its body weight in one meal— about 88 pounds (40 kg).

Tigers usually eat the meat from their prey first, followed by organs such as the heart and liver.

Night Hunters

It is dusk, and a hungry tiger stands motionless among the long grass, virtually invisible. It is watching and waiting for something to move and is ready to pounce.

Silent Attack

Tigers hunt mostly at night, dawn, or dusk, so they have to make good use of their excellent senses of sight, smell, and hearing. They also learn where prey is likely to be found. They patrol areas, such as **waterholes** and rivers, visiting several times a night. Sometimes, they wait beside tracks leading to a waterhole. When their prey is about 10–15 yards (meters) away, they charge forward. The tiger hits the prey animal with the full force of its large body, knocking it to the ground. It grips with its claws so the prey cannot escape. This sudden, silent attack is over in seconds.

 When a tiger finds its prey, it creeps up slowly from behind.

Death Bite

A small animal is killed with a single bite to the neck through the spinal cord, but a larger animal is **suffocated**. The tiger squeezes its throat for up to ten minutes until it is dead. Then, the tiger drags the dead animal under nearby bushes where it is out of sight. It eats as much as it can and then covers the rest. It returns over the next few days to finish its feast.

SUCCESS RATE

The tiger is an expert hunter, but only one in every 20 hunts ends in a kill. In areas where prey is in short supply, even fewer hunts are successful. Sometimes the animal gets away, and the tiger is not quick enough to chase it. Or other animals, such as monkeys and birds, warn nearby creatures of a tiger's approach.

This tiger has caught a spotted deer fawn. Adult tigers hunt at least once a week.

15

Living Alone

Tigers are **solitary** animals that live alone for much of the time. They come into contact with other tigers to mate, and females live with their cubs for a while. The area in which they live and hunt is called a **territory**.

Territory Rules

Once a female tiger has found her own suitable territory that has plenty of food, she keeps it for life. The size of a tiger's territory varies, depending on the type of habitat. In a dense jungle with lots of deer, a territory may cover just 8 square miles (20 sq km). But in the vast forests of China and Russia where there are few prey animals, a territory may reach more than 174 square miles (450 sq km). The male tiger usually establishes a territory that overlaps those of several females, but is well away from other males.

Sometimes a male tiger is chased off its territory by a stronger male.

TREE HUGGERS

Tigers like to leave their scent in places where other tigers can smell it. Sometimes, a tiger wraps its front legs around a branch and gives it a big hug. Then they rub their chest on the bark to leave a smell. This is about the height of the nose of another tiger.

Tigers rub their bodies and faces on trees to leave hairs and scent behind.

Marking the Boundaries

Tigers like to warn other tigers to stay away. They patrol the boundaries of their territory and mark boulders and trees with their urine. They use their claws to leave deep scratch marks on trees. Amazingly, this system works well, and there are few boundary disputes. Sometimes the males fight over a female, but usually they stay away from each other. The tiger may be one of the best hunters in the world, but it is not a great fighter. Tigers avoid fights because they could injure themselves. An injured tiger cannot hunt and is at risk of dying from starvation.

The Siberian Tiger

The tiger with the largest territory is the Siberian (or Amur) tiger of eastern Russia and northern China. These tigers live in the vast northern coniferous forests where prey animals are few and far between.

Keeping Warm

The Siberian tiger is the largest of all. It has thick fur, with long hair and a particularly thick ruff around its neck. This makes it look even bigger. Its cozy fur and layers of body fat help it survive the extremely cold winters where temperatures plunge to -50°F (-46°C). The tiger has extra hair between its paws for **insulation**. The Siberian tiger has fewer stripes than the Bengal tiger, and the stripes are brown rather than black. There is more white in the fur, too, which improves its camouflage against the snow. It is often confused with the white Bengal tiger.

The Siberian tiger has adapted to live in a cold climate.

Heat is trapped by almost 20,000 hairs in a single inch (about 3,000 hairs in a single sq cm) of skin

On the Decline

The number of Siberian tigers declined during the 1980s due to extensive **deforestation** and hunting. During the 1990s, the Siberian Tiger Project got underway. Scientists from Russia and the United States worked together to study tigers in their natural habitat. New tiger reserves were set up, and numbers increased.

There are now estimated to be about 400 Siberian tigers in the wild and the same number in **captivity**. In Russia, forests have been protected or replanted to attract prey animals, such as boar. Poaching bans have also helped to save tigers and their prey. But despite these huge conservation efforts, the Siberian tiger could become extinct in the wild within ten years.

This tiger has a much broader muzzle than the Bengal tiger.

About 50 percent of tiger cubs die before they are a year old, often because their mothers have been shot.

Tiger Talk

The roar of a tiger echoing through a forest is a sound that many animals dread. Tigers make other sounds, too, including groans, snarls, and grunts. But unlike other cats, tigers cannot purr.

Getting Attention

A tiger's roar tells other tigers to stay away. It is also a way of attracting a mate. When a tiger roars, its ears twist around so the white spot on the back of its ear can be seen. This may be a visual sign, telling another tiger that it is annoyed. Tigers do not roar very often, but when they want to impress a female, they are very noisy indeed!

A tiger's roar only lasts for a few seconds, but it is a chilling sound.

Moans, Growls, and Snarls

A mother tiger moans gently to her cubs to call them. She makes other sounds including a chuff, a type of snorting sound. Tigers that know each other make a chuff sound when they greet each other. They also rub their faces to spread scent (left). An aggressive, attacking tiger growls a warning. It hisses or spits, and swishes its tail from side to side. A defensive tiger bares its teeth and holds its tail low, near the ground.

LONG-DISTANCE RELATIONSHIPS

It is difficult to see far in a forest, so sound is a much better form of communication. A tiger's roar carries through the forest for more than 2 miles (3 km). This enables tigers to keep in contact over long distances.

This tiger is snarling with its ears flat against its head to say, "Stay away."

Tiger Cubs

A female tiger has her first cubs when she is about three or four years of age. The cubs stay with their mother for up to two years, when they are ready to live on their own. Then the female has another litter.

Helpless Cubs

A female tiger is pregnant for 16 weeks and gives birth to between one and four cubs. The cubs are born blind and helpless and weigh just 2.2 pounds (1 kg). They have small teeth and feed on their mother's milk. After ten days, their eyes open. They are too small to wander around the forest, so the mother leaves them hidden in a den, such as a thicket of dense shrubs, or in a small cave or crevice in the rocks. Sadly, only half the cubs will survive until their first birthday.

The female hides her young cubs in a den so they are less likely to be found by predators such as snakes, leopards, or jackals.

Hunting with Mother

When they are about two months old, the cubs leave the den and follow their mother through the forest. When they are larger, they are allowed to go hunting with her, to learn the skills of catching prey. By the time the young tigers are 18 months old, they are hunting on their own. Tigers stay with their mother until they are about two years old, when they are chased away by their mother and find territory of their own. Female tigers stay in the same area as their mother, but the males move much farther away.

TIGER EYES

Everybody thinks tigers have beautiful amber-colored eyes, but tiger cubs are born with bright blue eyes that gradually change color to amber. This happens in other mammals, too. Some dogs are born with bright blue eyes that change within a few weeks to brown, and human babies are often born with blue eyes that change color, too.

Play fighting is important because it teaches cubs how to hunt and fight.

Man-Eating Tigers

Tigers kill more people than either lions or leopards. During the nineteenth century, when there were many more tigers in Asia, tigers are thought to have killed hundreds of thousands of people. Today there are fewer tigers, and fewer attacks, but tigers are still feared.

Tiger Attack

Tigers do not normally attack people, unless they are threatened or are guarding their young. Sometimes, the attack may be a case of mistaken identity. A person who is bending over, for example, may look like a deer. Fortunately, **man-eating** tigers are rare. Hunger forces some old or injured tigers to attack people, especially if they come into close contact with the tiger's territory.

Tigers usually attack from behind. These men are wearing masks to scare any tigers away.

Dangerous Swamps

The tiger-attack capital of the world is the Sundarban swamps on the border of India and Bangladesh. This huge area is home to about 600 Bengal tigers that kill up to 100 people every year. Scientists are unsure why there are so many attacks because the tigers are healthy, and there is plenty of food. However, the people living near the swamps are very poor. Hunger forces them into the tiger's territory to find food. Sometimes, a hungry tiger leaves the swamp in search of goats and chickens in a village, and will attack people there, too, if the chance arises.

These men are trying to count tigers in the Sundarban swamps. They have a gun for protection.

Captured!

After a tiger attack, the local villagers usually go in search of the tiger to kill it. But because tigers are becoming rare, a man-eater may be caught and moved to a safer area, or taken to a zoo (below) where any injuries can be treated.

Tigers Under Threat

Tigers are at serious risk of becoming extinct. This **endangered** species has been losing its habitat and facing the threat of hunters. Although it is illegal to sell a tiger skin or use parts of a tiger's body to make a medicine, these trades continue, especially in countries such as China.

Protecting Tigers

A tiger's habitat can be protected by establishing reserves and national parks. However, hunting (or poaching) is still a huge threat. Poaching has wiped out tigers in reserves such as the Sariska tiger reserve in India. Although there are anti-poaching patrols, it is difficult to protect such a large area.

 Tourists pay to see tigers in nature reserves, which can help to fund more conservation work.

Zoo Animals

There are almost as many tigers living in zoos and wildlife parks as there are in the wild. Although it is better for tigers to be living wild, the zoos help to conserve rare tigers, such as the Sumatran and South China tiger. If numbers increase, it may be possible to release these tigers back into the wild. A small group of South China tigers, for example, are undergoing "re-wilding" training in South Africa where they are learning to hunt and fend for themselves, so they can be released back into the wild.

THE RAREST TIGER

There are fewer than 20 South China tigers left in the wild, and just 60 in zoos. In 1960, there were more than 4,000 living in China, but the tiger was declared to be a pest by the government because it attacked farm animals. It was hunted until there were virtually none left.

Tiger skins and medicines made from tiger bones and organs can still be found in shops in China.

Facts and Records

As top predators of the jungle, tigers are feared for their powerful paws, sharp claws, and ferocious bite. They are amazing in many ways.

Largest and Smallest

- The Siberian tiger is the largest of all the tigers. It is heavier and longer than a male lion, but not quite as tall.

- The Sumatran tiger is the smallest. The males weigh about 265 pounds (120 kg). That's similar to a female lion.

The Sumatran tiger is the smallest king of the cats.

Did You Know?

- A captive tiger can live for 20 years, but a wild tiger lives for just 10 to 15 years.

- It is impossible to count how many tigers are left in the wild, but experts estimate there are fewer than 6,000.

Tiger Cubs

- A young tiger cub grows quickly, gaining up to 3.5 ounces (100 g) in weight each day.

- Scientists think the white spots behind the ears of tigers help cubs to follow their mother through the shady forest.

Names and Numbers

- The Latin name for the tiger is *Panthera tigris*. The word *Panthera* comes from a Greek word meaning "hunter" while *tigris* is an Old Persian word meaning "fast" or "arrow-like."

- A group of tigers is called a streak.

- A tiger's paw prints are called pug marks. The pug mark of an adult tiger is about 6 inches (15 cm) long and 4 inches (11 cm) wide.

- A tiger can spend up to 18 hours sleeping.

Record-Breakers

- The South China tiger has the fewest stripes, while the Sumatran tiger has the most.

- One of the best-known man-eaters was a female Bengal tiger called Champawat. She was believed to have killed more than 400 people during the 1930s before she was killed by a hunter.

Body Facts

- Tigers have striped skin, not just striped fur.

- A tiger's tongue is covered with tiny, hard lumps that scrape meat off the bones of their prey.

- A tiger's saliva is an antiseptic. It is useful for cleaning their wounds.

- A tiger's night vision is six times better than a human's.

- A tiger's tail can be up to one-third of its body length. It helps the tiger to balance when running.

Glossary

camouflage
the colors and patterns on an animal's skin, fur, or feathers that help it blend with its surroundings, so that it is hard to see

canine
a sharp, pointed tooth used for gripping and seizing prey

captivity
when an animal is kept in a zoo or wildlife park

carnivore
an animal that eats meat

coniferous
an evergreen tree that has needles and produces cones

conservation
the protection of natural habitats, plants, and animals

deforestation
the cutting down of trees for wood to use, or to clear an area for building or agriculture

endangered
at risk of becoming extinct

extinct
no longer in existence, having died out

habitat
a particular place where plants and animals live, such as a tropical forest or desert

insulation
a material, such as fur or feathers, that traps heat

jungle
dense forest found in tropical parts of the world

mammal
an animal that feeds its young on milk and has hair on its body

man-eater
a tiger that has taken to attacking and eating people

poacher
a person who hunts animals illegally

predator
an animal that
hunts others
for food

prey
an animal that is
eaten for food
by another

reserve
an area that
is protected

solitary
living alone

species
a particular type
of animal, such
as a tiger

suffocate
prevent from
breathing

territory
an area where
an animal lives,
hunts, and breeds,
and which it may
defend against
others of its kind

tropical
an area or climate
that is warm and
often wet, close
to the equator
(the imaginary
line around the
Earth's middle)

waterhole
an area where
water collects,
forming a
large pond

zodiac
a type of calendar

Index

Web Finder

WWF Tiger Overview
www.worldwildlife.org/species/finder/tigers/index.html
Learn about different kinds of tigers.

Kids for Tigers
www.kidsfortigers.org
Find out about tigers and how you can help save them.

Tiger Project
www.wcs.org/saving-wildlife/big-cats/tiger.aspx
Find out about the Wildlife Conservation Society's work to save the tigers.

Sumatran Tiger Trust
www.tigertrust.info/sumatran_tiger_home.asp
Find out how you can help save the Sumatran Tiger.

Tiger: Photos, Video, Facts, E-Card
kids.nationalgeographic.com/Animals/CreatureFeature/Tiger
Examine facts, photos, videos, and other information about tigers.